BALI
MYSTIQUE

Elora Hardy

BALI
MYSTIQUE

ASSOULINE

INTRODUCTION

ARRIVAL

The coconut palms swing from the force of the air, a wave of warmth pours into the cabin as the airplane doors open. Stepping down the air stairs, welcomed by wizened plumeria trees that frame the carved-stone gateways. A bustle of ramps and stamps and baggage, then the drive home to Ubud, a gradient shifting from grays to green, finally immersed in stretches of rice fields that whip past like deep inhales. Perhaps a glimpse of a volcano among the clouds and electrical wires. Once I'm in the village, the green becomes punctuated by flowers tumbling toward me over courtyard walls. Stopping at a roadside café, I plunge into a pile of steaming rice heaped with veggies, coconuts and meats. The heat of the spices rushes to my head, bringing me home. These are my strongest memories of Bali from my teenage years in the 1990s—coming home.

The island of Bali is at the heart of the Indonesian archipelago, which drapes below mainland Southeast Asia like a coral necklace. Many waves of cultures and religions have rippled through these islands, brought by seafarers, traders and priests. Within what is now a primarily Islamic country, Bali is Hindu Dharma, a form of Hinduism that is entwined with Buddhist and animist traditions and linked to a lineage of nobles and artisans from the Majapahit civilization, with roots extending far back into the Austronesian migrations. I grew up on the outskirts of several kingdoms where local history and mystery

Daily life in Tenganan, one of the ancient villages on the island of Bali.
Following pages: A Balinese welcome, with an offering of frangipani, invites visitors to slow down and acclimate to the leisurely pace of the island.

blurred. My European and Balinese fairy tales merged with real-life travel adventures overheard from visitors passing through, mingling to become my story of Bali.

HOME

Bali is woven into my identity, a concept of separateness and belonging, love and nostalgia. Bali is my home. My Canadian parents stopped here in 1975 while on a yearlong around-the-world adventure. As they journeyed by train across Java, Bali was initially just a perfunctory stop in what they believed was an overexposed tourist destination. Despite their preconceptions, they soon fell in love with Bali and, after several years in a rented cottage overlooking the Campuhan gorge, and having bought kitchenware, realized this was home.

Our front porch was a way station for friends of friends from around the world. In the years before we had a telephone, people would arrive before the letter that let us know to expect them. They would ask for travel tips, join us for a sunset drink and then hike up to the rice fields to rent a bungalow for a week. In the following years, I wouldn't be surprised to see them return again and again, a few inevitably befriending a farmer or a prince, starting a business and staying forever.

BLISS

Upon arriving in Bali, after becoming adjusted to the humidity, visitors are met with another quintessential characteristic of the island: positivity. An immersion to help relearn how to smile at every opportunity. The tattooed man on a motorbike, scowling against the glare of the sun, smiles the moment you make eye contact and turns to reveal a baby draped across his lap. Dads from the village hanging out on the stoop with their toddlers, watching the world go by, smile as you pass. Head into the rice fields, a toothless grandma pauses in her work to grin and nod when you catch her eye. Greet her in Bahasa Indonesia, and she will light up. If you crack a joke in Bahasa Bali, she will beam with delight.

They say the Balinese language has several words for happiness because there is a distinction between individual and communal happiness, although both are highly valued. Balinese culture is constantly and intentionally striving toward the balancing of three realms: people, nature and the gods. Achieving balance in any of these realms is deemed important and seems to contribute to the intangible sparkle of the island, as if by shifting the focus off the individual there is more cause for joy. A well-balanced brand of happiness.

BALANCE

Blessings abound in Bali. Ceremonies, festivals and celebrations are all an ongoing bid to appease all forces, both good and evil. Every northeast corner of every room, building, compound, field and intersection features a shrine. Simple or elaborate offerings are made at each, depending on the day. But look closely and you realize that temple gates are not all carved with graceful deities. Many are ferocious, with fanged teeth and an intimidating glare. In Balinese cosmology, the demon queen, Rangda, is a gloomy, vengeful avatar associated with the Hindu goddess Durga, her drooping breasts almost as long as her spiky tongue. By showing embodiments of evil, by building temples and holding ceremonies to appease them, the Balinese keep the world in balance. And for those of us watching, our interior demons, usually suppressed, can be acknowledged. Rangda and other statues, shrines and holy trees are wrapped in *poleng* cloth, an assortment of checker prints that combine black and white as a reminder that good, evil and everything in between are all constantly at play, so it is essential to keep them in balance.

Following pages: A sitting area, designed by Linda Garland, with a view of the ocean at a Minang house in Candi Dasa.

THE ELEMENTS OF BALI

WATER

Monsoon rains pour onto the mountains, filling the Danau Batur crater lake.

Rivers wind their way from the center,

outward in all directions toward the coasts.

Holy water pours from rock at Tirta Empul, Tirta Gangga,

and a thousand other springs.

Centuries of traders, farmers and courtiers flow into Bali from the west.

Now visitors pour out of the airport and trickle north.

People and water cycle round and round through Waterbom's joyful waterslides.

Seawater permeates the water tables, Mantra environmental engineers push back.

FIRE

The taste of spice is how we internalize fire,

Maya Kerthyasa tends to her grandmother's wood-burning stove.

Shadow-puppet plays at midnight temple ceremonies.

A dance where a man, while in a trance, walks on fire.

Life does not end with cremation, but rather it begins the process of reincarnation,

In between are transitions, glimpses of shadows and spirits—the supernatural.

The lava once flowed all around Mount Agung's Besakih Temple.

Raw food Alchemy and yoga under a copper dome.

In the town of Pejeng, a bronze drum—the moon—fell to Earth.

EARTH

Stimulants grow on the slopes: artisanal coffees, chocolates, kombucha, beer.

A view of the fields while sipping on green at Rüsters:

an almond matcha latte, or a cocktail made with leaves.

Hands turn blue picking and dipping indigo

in the mountains at Tian Taru, while Kalpa Taru designs fine, carved teak.

Every homestead has a back garden, an abundance of mysterious plants

coloring the cloth at Cinta Bumi and woven into Threads of Life.

Tableware and artworks at Gaya Ceramic are earth turned by fire into stone,

then coated with metallic glaze and the memory of burnt-off rice husks.

Terra shows us that a simple clay pot can safely filter water for everyone.

Tales of priestly initiation rites, navigating from the mountain to the sea

through tunnels in the bedrock.

Volcanic earth, coral cliffs, stone crumbling into sand.

WIND

White herons of Petulu.

Skies swirling with kites during the dry season.

Louise Despont draws the flow of air.

Masuk angin a common local malady, meaning "the wind has entered me."

The Painted Alphabet gives us a glimpse into an unseen world

of spirits traversing clouds and waves.

Tendrils of incense smoke twirl upwards from offerings everywhere.

Fireflies, only where the air is clean enough, sparkle in the night.

ALCHEMICAL ISLAND: LAYERS OF LOVE AND LAVA

Bali is a magnetic, alchemical island. Along with an international assortment of tourists and travelers, it has always attracted creatives: artists, entrepreneurs, writers, performers. People searching for something more than a holiday. From healing to hedonism, there is an energy here that defies the stereotype of a serene tropical paradise. Bali is conducive to relaxation, but it is more likely to inspire you: to swim, write, climb, learn, revive, create.

Visitors run the risk of falling in love. And it's not necessarily up to you to choose: Bali has a say. She either embraces you and catches your heart, or tumbles you around and sends you on a new path. Bali has a special kind of attraction. Being volcanic in the physical sense, Bali is also literally magnetic. The center of the Balinese universe is its highest and holiest peak, the majestic volcano Mount Agung. Much of this island rose from the sea floor in a series of eruptions. Over the eons, layers of magma spilled forth and turned to soil, rippled with rivers and carved out rice fields. In contrast to the black volcanic soil of central Bali, the high white cliffs of Uluwatu reveal layers of limestone lifted from the ocean floor. The land itself is made up of contrast. It builds up like those layers of magma, coral and bone becoming limestone, existing through the eras of international occupation from ancient times to today.

CELEBRATION: DANCING ON THE PERIPHERY

We lived in the no-man's-land between village and town center, in the former home of Walter Spies and Rudolf Bonnet, part of the first wave of European artists. As foreigners we felt welcomed but were not expected to participate in the local celebrations, so my parents made our own festivities. For one party we made scarecrows out of bamboo and thatch, with woven hats, coconut breasts and ratty T-shirts. We paraded them up to the sugarcane fields of Nenek Tebu, a local farmer who had a special love of scarecrows.

Each Halloween, we created costumes and visited restaurants with candlelit pumpkins, asking confused waiters for treats. These memories are not to be outdone by the time David Bowie dressed as Santa Claus at a Christmas party held at the Café Lotus, circa 1990. "Have you been to Bali? My God, do they dress. Every day of the week there's a celebration," Bowie once quipped about the island's penchant for amusement. There were other families like us in Ubud with cross-cultural heritage. For example, Bowie's hosts were Amir Rabik, from Indonesia, and Linda Garland, an interior designer for the stars, from Ireland. At their house parties, colorful personalities adorned in bohemian fashions were strewn across woven mats under lace umbrellas.

SANDS: RIDING THE TIDES

Bali is a paradox, encouraging both mindful mornings and indulgent nights. By the year 2000, the Seminyak Beach area ignited as a hub of fashion, music and hedonism. Long before there were clubs, resident expats hosted and organized full-moon parties, white parties, red parties, house parties. Also long a surf spot, the town begins its days with meditative moments on the waves or yoga mats at dawn, vegan-café hopping, an afternoon at the shops or spa. Sunset is time for beers on the beach or cocktails at Mari Beach Club, the latest and loveliest addition to the sunset strip. The serious crowd might go home for a nap, then time to get dressed for a ten p.m. dinner perhaps at the classic Ku De Ta, which was among the first sophisticated beachfront clubs in Bali. Earlier, in 1987, Double Six opened, named for its hours: six p.m. to six a.m. Its millennium New Year's bubble party was featured on page one of *The New York Times* the following day.

All these layers of identity, clusters of activity, clubs, shops, restaurants, villas, embedded within and between traditional village life, fluctuate throughout

Following pages: (*left*) Diamond Beach on nearby Penida Island. (*right*) A swimwear editorial photographed in Bali for *Cleo* magazine, 2005.

the year with the waves of expats, travelers and tourists. These various cycles, like the two of the many parallel and overlapping calendar systems of Bali, reinforce the understanding that we are inevitably traveling round and round through cycles of reincarnation. Good and bad, insider and outsider, a balancing act.

SAMADHI

Coastal vibes are born from the seabed and moon tides, which conspire to create the waves that draw surfers from around the world. The beaches range in extremes: pure white coral sand of Nyang Nyang, Sindhu Sanur's coarse golden grains, fine black sand at Keramas and volcanic mica sparkling at Lipah. Surfer culture began here in the 1970s, based out of thatch shacks on the cliffs. Gerry Lopez, one of the earliest and most famous surfers to explore Bali, has said he believes he reached a state of *samadhi* (deep meditation) while surfing Uluwatu. He is not alone in this experience, and it's why the waves here have become some of the most sought-after in the world. These far-south cliff towns of Bali, a longtime insider secret, with outposts of charming cottages like Mu Bali and a small dappling of exclusive hotels, have been growing recently, welcoming a community of surfers who prefer the dry winds. During the first uncertain months of Covid in 2020, most travelers left Bali, and many expat residents returned to their domestic homes, but some, like surf champion Kelly Slater and F1 driver Lewis Hamilton, chose to escape to Bali, retreating to Uluwatu Surf Villas and the enlightening waves.

REGENERATION

What washes up with the tides? Among the playfulness and industry of business, both big and small, the ocean is calling attention to the excesses happening on land. Trash appears within Bali's rivers mixed with the river sand that fuels concrete construction of hotels and villas. Or it floats here from other islands and becomes entangled in the surf. In the absence of significant government intervention, restoration activism is percolating locally from unexpected places. Sungai Watch, Bye Bye Plastic Bags, and Plastic Exchange are world-renowned, home-grown efforts emerging to gather and repurpose waste, to disrupt the cycle of use. Scientists at the Biosphere Foundation have been working to restore the coral reefs. While tourism contributes to the problem, improvements are being made in this industry as well. The hospitality sector is reinventing and reintegrating. A decade ago Potato Head redefined the concept of the beach club, and now its founder, Ronald Akili, continues to challenge the status quo with Desa Potato Head, a "creative village with a global feel." It is an audiophile event space, gallery and curated library, along with being an award-winning hotel at a crossroads of international design and craftsmanship by OMA. Its mission is to invite and enable people to have good times and make the world a better place, understanding that life is a balance. Good Life, Good Vibes, Do Good.

COCONUT BOUNTY: BEYOND THE SYMBOLIC

Overlaid on the beautiful landscape of Bali is a graciousness of culture and character so pleasant that visitors, and even colonists, have long recognized it as something worth protecting and participating in. Many visitors are first called to Bali by the coconut coasts, pastoral tropical scenes of swaying palms above idyllic beaches. Before the villages of Kuta, Legian and Seminyak grew and fused into one stretch of commerce, they were villages of palm groves along the sunset-facing coast. The sun rises over the sleepy reefs of Sanur, where coconut groves were transformed into the Hotel Tandjung Sari and the elegant estates at Batujimbar. The island's tallest building, at ten stories, is found a short distance up the coast. This building prompted Bali's height regulation: A building cannot be taller than a coconut tree (about fifty feet).

Following pages: (*left*) The *candi bentar* (split gateway) of Pura Penataran Agung Lempuyang, a Balinese Hindu temple, or *pura*, situated on the slope of Mount Lempuyang. (*right*) A wedding performance of the Oleg dance, also known as "the dance of the bumblebees."

ABUNDANCE

More than just an icon on a postcard, the coconut tree is used in its entirety in Bali: a nutritious fruit that holds drink and food, sweet and savory, sacred and mundane. Shells used for bowls, leaves used for mats and traditional books, wood used for shelter and ornamentation. It's essentially a one-stop shop, embodying abundance and omnipresent in daily life. Climbing, husking, harvesting, cracking, grating, pleating. A fruit to prepare and cook together, to feast on together, to pray over.

The Indonesian word *ramé* means something that is simultaneously chaotic and joyful; crowded, but with a positive connotation of togetherness; busy, but constructive. A representation of how being a part of something is more desirable than being alone. In Bali, solitude is defined as lonely isolation. Togetherness—and community—is at the heart of this culture of abundance.

A sense of pleasant abundance has permeated Bali's international reputation, attracting creatives and seekers of knowledge, who in turn propel that identity. Ubud Readers & Writers festival was founded by Janet DeNeefe with the explicit intention of highlighting the island's creative energy. Ubud, named after the Balinese word for medicine, has become synonymous with wellness, ever since the founding of Kadek Gunarta and Meg Pappenheim's BaliSpirit Festival, attracting yogis looking to eat, pray and love.

NURTURING

In the early twentieth century, the first European artists in Bali shared glimpses with the broader world of a culture and a community worth visiting. Paintings and films depicting casually bare-breasted women in the marketplace enticed early European travelers like Charlie Chaplin. By the middle of the twentieth century, Balinese women were covering up with *kebaya* blouses, either in compliance with Dutch instruction or to guard against the sexualizing Western gaze. Bare breasts made a reappearance on Kuta Beach for a time in the 1970s and '80s, spearheaded simultaneously by hippies and Brazilians playing paddleball. But the breast as a sexual symbol does not translate across cultures. As a child witnessing the days when village grandmothers still took on or off their blouses depending only on their own sense of comfort and inclination, my sister Carina went on to create Elppin, breast-inspired jewelry. As a woman, she had been searching for a way to reclaim the nipple, to both armor and adorn it. Though existing within a clearly patriarchal structure, the feminine identity in Bali is proud and strong, practical and competent. Women are often responsible for maintaining their family's financial stability. Bali has not been immune to international standards of modesty, fashion and health care, often adopting external practices, but in some small instances Bali is on the forefront. Midwife Robin Lim, a CNN Hero, founded the Bumi Sehat birthing clinic, addressing the specific needs of the local women. Here, the cycle of life is integrated into both individual and communal rhythms. Across the field from the clinic, in a restaurant called Mother, tired parents are likely to find themselves able to eat with both hands as their baby is scooped up and passed happily among the cooing waiters, a common occurrence in Bali.

RICE CYCLES

My de facto childhood caretaker, Pak Made, a farmer by trade, loved to entertain me by concocting unexpected foods. A shiny leaf soaked in water turned to gelatin, and then, mixed with coconut milk and palm sugar, it became a delicious slimy green drink. We would go "fishing" for dragonflies using bamboo sticks with tree sap on the end, then he would fry them up with diced ginger flowers. Spotting a wasp nest up on the ceiling, he would extract a wriggling larva and roast it briefly on the edge of a flame. There

Following pages: The rolling green rice fields of Seseh.

were some fruits and roots that he would identify as safe but not recommend, telling tales of hungrier times when he would sneak them from neighbors' gardens. As the pandemic took hold in 2020, Pak Made moved from downtown Ubud to live in my family compound, becoming the guardian of our garden beds and resident grandfather to our kids. Contemplating the possibility of more hard times ahead, he speculated whether people would be turning to the many unacknowledged bounties of the forest again. He expressed this thought with pride for his generation, still alive to guide. Within the living memory of many Balinese elders, rice has gone from delicacy to staple. Today, every Balinese meal is centered around it, the texture and flavor of all other food are best when it is offset against the smooth, satisfying, mouth-filling simplicity of white rice.

FUSION

Visitors often marvel at the pristine and well-preserved ancient culture of Bali, but that's not the full story. I see a culture, like bamboo, flexible enough to remain itself while changing with times, the grace to welcome outsiders while retaining its integrity. The central mountain ranges and jungles beyond helped slow the outside influence and delayed colonial control for centuries, allowing the continuity of culture, with skills and traditions layering and strengthening over time. Much of what we notice on the surface isn't entirely local, original or ancient. Rice agriculture came from mainland Asia, chilies are traded from the Americas, gods' names were brought from India, some of the styles of temple and palace elements were adopted from China. In recent history, local dances have been reinvented, such as the famous *kecak,* a collaboration between a Balinese dancer and a German artist from the 1930s. Ubud painters who sought to establish their painting style consulted with Dutch artist Rudolf Bonnet. Ogoh-Ogoh statues are said to have first joined the Ngrupuk carnival in 1983, in celebration of Indonesia recognizing Nyepi, the Bali day of silence, as a national holiday. As in most cultures, transplantation and evolution are inevitable, but Bali has withstood, embracing outside influences but incorporating them into its own culture, without being overwhelmed.

ARTISTRY

Once a wild, forested landscape, Bali began to be tamed two thousand years ago as farmers carved it into rice terraces and food forests that still sweep across the lowland plains. Though the original forests held a secret edible bounty, consistent agriculture would allow for a new rhythm of culture to emerge, where specialization and artistry could thrive. Rice and many other crops cycled through the fields, some steeply terraced and others expansive. Villages situated agricultural zones in between and behind each household, a family fruit forest. There were enough good times that, between planting and harvest, the months of leisure became busy with activity. Though calm, there is no tradition of stillness here or idle hands. Young dancers impossibly flex their elegant fingers, otherwise immobile priests ring prayer bells, groups of women talk as they weave, craftsmen's hands alternate between carving tools and cigarettes. For hundreds of years, prior to Indonesia's independence, priests and kings patronized and controlled the artists' guilds. Districts of stone and wood carvers developed, containing entire hamlets specializing in birds or flowers or human representations. Poppies Lane in Kuta was once home to the most skilled goldsmith guilds of Southeast Asia. I spent afternoons at Made's Warung restaurant while my mother, Penny Berton, visited goldsmiths, who between carving priestly rings realized my mother's interpretation of a balanced universe, with lotuses reading upward and jeweled serpents swirling down. Along the main streets of Sukawati, hundreds of workshops sell gilded-silver offering bowls, earrings fit for a

Following pages: (*left*) Annabel North-Lewis rinses off in the outdoor shower at Karma Kandara. (*right*) Nungnung waterfall is a hidden gem in Bali.

Majapahit princess, as well as replicas of runway pieces. Over just the past half century, Tampaksiring specialized in bone carving. In Batubulan ("Stone Moon") village, a menagerie of carvings line the streets. Every creature is immortalized in stone. Each palace, temple and shrine is tended, the preservation and reinvention of which is a point of generational pride.

BAMBOO VISIONS FOR THE FUTURE

Bamboo has been utilized across the tropical regions of the world for thousands of years. This wild grass grows among the steep ravines of Bali and is as ubiquitous as coconut and rice. Born on a bamboo mat, cremated in a bamboo pyre and, in between, fishing and cooking and praying and shopping and sleeping with bamboo, which is built and woven into myriad forms. Islands like Bali were likely first reached by bamboo rafts. Growing to full maturity in just three to four years, the plant regenerates soil and replenishes underground water sources as it grows.

The bamboo bug first bit our neighbor Linda Garland while she clutched a big, beautiful *Dendrocalamus asper* pole serving as the outrigger of a *jukung* canoe. Extolling the virtues of this overlooked material became her life's work, creating the Environmental Bamboo Foundation, a dedication that her son Arief Rabik carries on today with the Bamboo Village Initiative, which strengthens communities and the forests around them.

GREEN

My father, John Hardy, was a self-proclaimed wood man until his friend Linda "banged me over the head with bamboo enough times," so that when he and my stepmom, Cynthia, stepped away from their jewelry business to focus on their next ambitious project—founding Green School—it was the only material that could possibly live up to the name. They assembled a team to create an entire campus almost exclusively from treated bamboo. Constructed with such artistry and beauty that over the coming decade families around the world were inspired to visit and enroll. For many families, a "sabbatical year abroad" turns into founding or funding businesses here.

I was the next to fall for bamboo's spell. At twenty-eight, after fourteen years away, I traded New York for Bali while starting a long-distance marriage with my husband, Rajiv. To build Green School, a new technical and stylistic vocabulary of architecture had been created, one that could have taken shape only in Bali, building on the experience of a few brilliant international sparks. Every village man in Bali is adept at working with bamboo. However, in the absence of an exact vocabulary or even precedent, the rules, processes and systems of bamboo architecture had to be invented along the way. At our workshop, Bamboo Pure, we put a whole new industry into motion for harvesting, testing and treating. After which, at the Ibuku design studio, we learned to listen to the material and take into consideration what it wanted to become. Now Ibuku Studio designs internationally with mixed materials, designing spaces that provoke us to become who we wish to be.

GIFT

Ibuku and Bamboo Pure together have created over two hundred unique structures, across Bali and beyond, and also birthed what has been adopted as a new style for design in Bali. Curving bamboo buildings are now intrinsic to this destination, but it's a design vocabulary that we created in the past two decades. Bali is at the forefront of an international bamboo movement, so widespread that my brother Orin and his wife, Maria, launched Bamboo U to share our knowledge of bamboo with others around the world. Humanity has spent tens of thousands of years building structures to protect ourselves

Following pages: A scene filmed in Bali from *Morning of the Earth* (1972), a classic surf film about surfers in search of the perfect wave.

66 Bali was a surfer's paradise, which at the time was unknown to anyone but a few traveling nomads. The natural beauty of the island was truly spectacular, plus the surf was always great and uncrowded. It was pure bliss. For a surfer, it was heaven on earth. 99

Albert Falzon, *filmmaker*

from the outside world, and as a result, we began to shut ourselves off entirely. What if we could remember what it was like to be a part of nature? In a time of climate change and material scarcity, it is our responsibility to create an inspiring alternative aspiration.

Bamboo is a shining light of possibility. Imagine you could grow the materials for a whole home, or a whole skyscraper, or even a whole city, within four years? This material lets us attain abundance rather than scarcity. Beyond just being sustainable, bamboo proves that a green and beautiful future is possible. Its bountiful growth also parallels Balinese culture: resilient because of its ability to be flexible, maintaining its identity despite the pressures to conform. My kids, while in kindergarten at Green School, had a semester called "Gifts of the Earth," in which they learned about natural resources and how to see themselves as part of this whole. I see bamboo as an expression of Bali—an offering to the world.

WATER: FLOW AND BLESSING

In Bali, water pours in rivulets across the landscape, and adapting its flow has engaged the people in a dance that has formed the culture. While the villages and towns are often set on flat or gently sloping terrain, between them are ripping pleats, deep winding river valleys, mellowing near the coast. While the majority of attention centers on the beach towns, many travelers don't make it inland. Those who do find the joys of freshwater. Canyoning down from crater lakes, waterfall hunting, freshwater pools set into jungle cliffs, spas and water temples. Water in Bali is a shared resource and at the heart of Agama Tirta, the religion of water. While on a riverside walk, you are likely to encounter a young family doing their laundry and gathering water at a spring. Or a grandpa cooling down in the river, scrubbing his heels with a rock. Or kids on Google Maps chasing waterfalls by scooter.

DEMOCRACY

The Balinese are masters of water distribution. A UNESCO study involving computer simulations found that the Jatiluwih rice terraces, a system thousands of years old, could not be improved upon. It is not just a matter of planting and harvesting. Rice agriculture requires both spring and river water from deep ravines to be strategically redirected to reach fields miles downstream. Hand-carved water tunnels line a landscape already perforated with underground water channels that emerge in the cliffs as springs. This means water moves through and along the periphery of many villages, each in coordination with the others, across borders. The water is strategically diverted according to cycles embedded in the religious and ceremonial calendars, at times superseding politics. Each member of the *subak,* the watershed management system, has equal say regardless of wealth or caste, making it one of the oldest democratic systems in the world. Within a world of often warring kingdoms, the *subak* social system of cooperation among farmers has operated for more than a thousand years.

Now part of the democratic Republic of Indonesia, Bali has echoes of nobility, priestly knowledge and artist guilds, in tandem with the next generation: youth trained in hospitality flocking to cruise ships; professionals and developers from neighboring islands seeking more creative opportunities; entrepreneurs, chefs and artists all looking for their place in the world.

CLEANSING

The spirit of equitability evident in water allocation extends to blessings as well: A Balinese priest will bless anyone, regardless of their belief system, without any agenda or shadow of proselytization. There's a sense that with enough offerings, prayer and good intention, anything can be washed away— at least briefly, as karma reminds us that not everything is up to us.

THIRST QUENCHING

Everyone first comes to Bali thirsty for something, and then the aromatic heat perpetuates it. A pause in the shade and a sip from a coconut go a long way to soothe midday fatigue, but then that thirst inevitably resurfaces, whether from the spiciness of a local lunch, the exertion of a rice-field walk or the intensity of the firelight at a dance performance. The underlying desires are universal: for beauty, calm, intensity, self-expression, self-discovery. Looking to be refreshed or cleansed. Partly to do with whether you find yourself stuck in traffic behind a truck or a procession. Whether you find yourself inhaling exhaust or incense. Whether you choose Coca-Cola or coconut water. Some people come intending to love it here but seem to get washed right out of Bali. And then there are the lucky ones who find themselves in the flow, under the magnetic spell of the island.

Every time people ask me what it was like to grow up in Bali, I'm at a loss. How could I sum up such a privilege concisely? The depth of love and complexity I feel for this place are the same as many feel for their hometown, while at the same time exponentially filtered and nostalgic.

What did Bali mean to me growing up? A space for adventure, to run through the fields, down into the valley. Where we, as my mother phrased it, created more than jewelry, but melted minerals into memories, and wove the castles of the future out of grass. An intense immersion, of being embraced and somehow of being lifted up on the crest of a wave. To have an idea, water it and realize it. Life is a dance, and Bali is a magnifier and a microcosm of who we are. How we treat Bali is how we treat the world. If Bali receives us, if we can find a way into the dance, then we have glimpsed paradise.

Girls dressed to perform a traditional Balinese dance. Manipulated SX-70 Polaroid photograph by Hans Hoefer.

66 To me, Bali feels like the center of the surf world. 99

Tim Russo, *co-founder of the Drifter Surf shops*

66 **The real underlying magic of Bali and Uluwatu was just that … magic. Balinese culture incorporates lots of black magic and white magic. There was a pervading energy that seemed to percolate not only into the waves but also into everything and everyone there.** 99

Gerry Lopez, *surfer and journalist*

" We first moved to Bali just ready to relax and watch grass grow, to raise a family, surf and enjoy the simple freedoms life has to offer. "

George Gorrow, *hotelier*

66 Bali is a very special place— this tiny island, brimming with creativity, a hot spot for stylish travelers from around the world, interesting designers, a genuine artisan culture. 99

Gail Elliott, *model*

" Don't talk about heaven if you've never been to Bali. "

Toba Beta, *writer*

"There is nature there, both in man and landscape, which is terribly important to me."

Walter Spies, *artist*

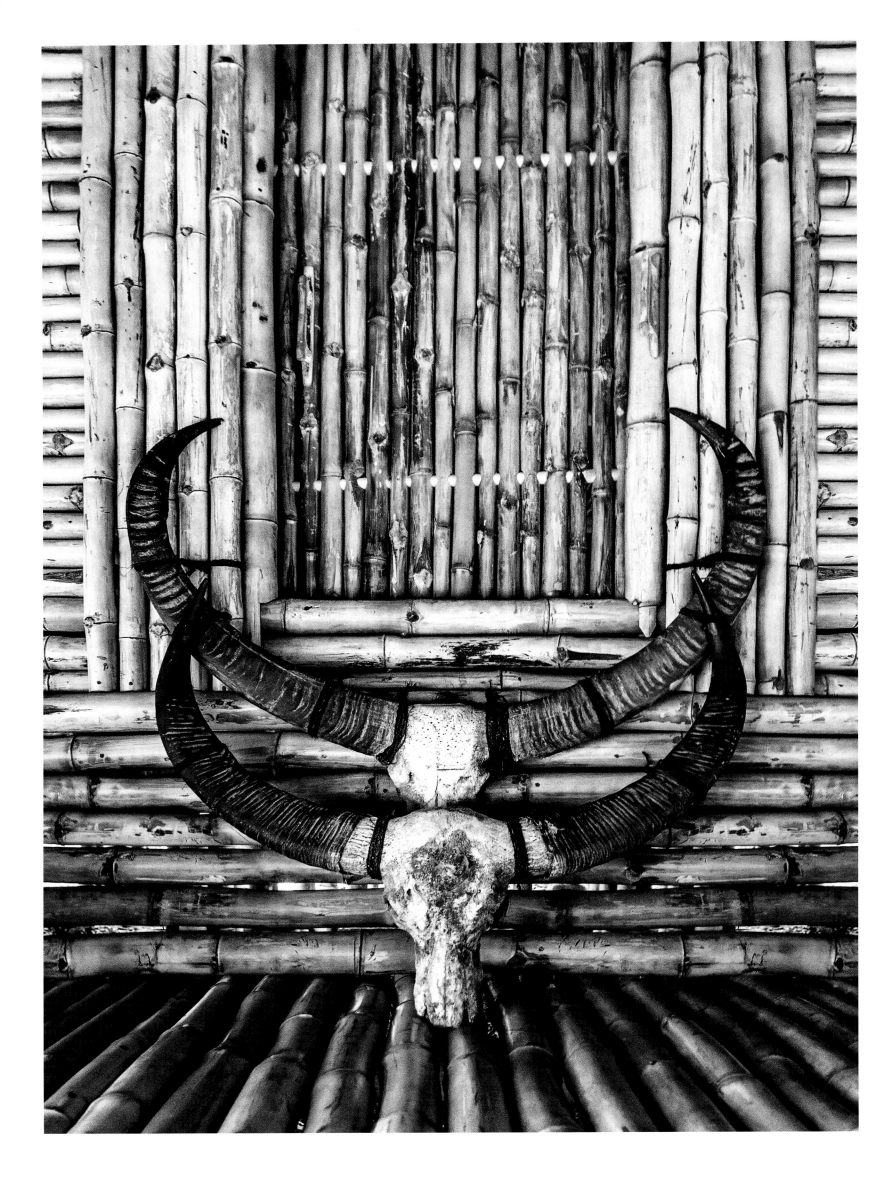

"The spirit of Bali is felt, seen, and tasted, permeating both body and mind."

Duncan Murray Kirk, *writer*

"The soul of Bali is unhurried. "

Lionel Shriver, *writer*

"My love affair with this land was influenced by the abundance of water. "

Linda Garland, *designer*

66 In Bali, life is a rhythmic, patterned unreality of pleasant, significant movement, centered in one's own body to which all emotions long ago withdrew. 99

Margaret Mead, *anthropologist*

"There's a certain something—a wild, spangled energy—that once saturated Bali as tangibly as its own tropical humidity. **"**

Diana Darling, *writer*

"Life, religion, and art all converge in Bali. They have no word in their language for 'artist' or 'art.' Everyone is an artist."

Anaïs Nin, *writer*

66 The finest view was that in front of the temple façade, where were stationed the band, men and women with their festive gongs, their stringed instruments and flutes, and, in front, the dancing girls in dazzling gold brocade and handsome adornments of fragrant temple flowers, tastefully arranged between the golden rays of the pearl-studded diadems. Now our eyes fell on the long, narrow hands, so infinitely full of expression in the dance. **99**

Charlie Chaplin, *comic actor and filmmaker*

"When I moved to Bali I was determined not to be one of those artists who paint old women with offerings and fruit. I shut off Bali—but Bali had seeped in, through the cracks."

Ashley Bickerton, *artist*

"I hope to convey a grounded sense of mystery and wonder. Anyone who comes to Bali will tell you that there is a certain magic in the air here."

Michael Dean Morgan, *photographer*

CAPTIONS

Off the coast of the Uluwatu Surf Villas, surfers from all over the world brave the ten-to-twelve-foot waves. A true surf mecca.

Left: Austin A40 Devon automobile beneath the palms of Bali.

Right: Amankila hotel offers a view of a temple perched on a verdant cliff.

Located in Seminyak, Potato Head Beach Club is one of the thoughtfully designed sites that make up the Desa Potato Head village.

Left: Motorbikes abound in Bali.

Right: Annely Bouma photographed by Stefano Galuzzi in Bali for *D: La Repubblica* magazine, 2020.

Crate Cafe has been serving the Canggu community since 2014.

Surfing is part of the daily routine in Bali.

Left: Balinese water purification ceremony in Klungkung Regency. Photographed by John Huba.

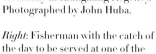

Right: Fisherman with the catch of the day to be served at one of the restaurants at Desa Potato Head.

Sunset over Penida Island, fifteen miles southeast of Bali.

Surfers refuel with coconut water at a surf shack.

The Pasir Putih Beach Club features alang-alang grass roofs alongside other natural architecture in order to fit harmoniously into the landscape.

Left: Discovering the beaches of Bali by horseback.

Right: The Lawn, a beach club in the heart of Canggu Beach, offers a captivating view of the Indian Ocean.

Flora, Taina and Diah—the next generation of female Indonesian surfers—head into the water to catch some waves.

Portrait of a Balinese "grommet," a young surfer, at Double Six Beach in Seminyak.

Traveling by vintage Volkswagen through the diverse topography of Bali.

Left: Sanur Beach, one of the first resort areas in Bali, 1971.

Right: A quick set of beach volleyball.

Bali caters to those leading an active lifestyle. There is no shortage of activities to choose from.

Brian Shimansky photographed by Mitchell Nguyen McCormack for *DA MAN Style*, 2015.

Left: Yocta Pratrista photographed in Bali by Cyril "C-reel" Saulnier for a Maison Mata campaign.

Right: Brian Shimansky in Indonesia photographed by Mitchell Nguyen McCormack, 2015.

View from Uluwatu Temple, located at the edge of a cliff overlooking the Indian Ocean.

Sparkling waters off the coast of Bali.

Local surfers pose with their boards on a beach in Sanur.

Left: Healthy lunch bowl with a smoothie at Drifter Cafe Uluwatu.

Right: Handcrafted MYC surfboard, painted by local artist Wayan Merta, at Drifter Surf shop.

Left: Bali has become a premier surfing destination due to its warm water, budget-friendly cost of living and impressive waves, which can be surfed year-round.

Right: Louis Grassell photographed by Cyril "C-reel" Saulnier for Mouty Paris.

Surfers Tyler Warren, Creed McTaggart and Dave Rastovich photographed in Bali for a Billabong campaign.

The swell of the decade, off the coast of the Bukit Peninsula. The waves were between thirty to forty feet.

Edelson House, designed by Cheong Yew Kuan in Bali.

Cara Delevingne in the John Hardy spring 2015 campaign.

Located on the Bukit Peninsula, the Edelson home was designed to take full advantage of the spectacular vistas.

Taking in the mesmerizing tropical atmosphere of Bali.

The rooms at Four Seasons Resort Bali at Jimbaran Bay are the epitome of indoor-outdoor living.

Kedungu Beach is a popular surf spot, with a long stretch of black sand.

Left: Editorial in Bali for *Men's Vogue China*.

Right: Copper House at Bambu Indah is a private sanctuary overlooking the Ayung River.

Brutalist tropical home in a rice-field setting and designed by architecture firm Patisandhika and designer Dan Mitchell.

Left: Aura House at Green Village is built from bamboo.

Right: Villa in the jungle treetops of Ubud, built using reclaimed wood from traditional Javanese homes, known as *joglos*.

Green School Bali was conceived as a new model for sustainable education in 2006 by John and Cynthia Hardy. The construction of the campus led to many innovations in bamboo architecture and engineering.

An incredible work of bamboo architecture, the Arc at Green School was completed on Earth Day in 2021 by Ibuku, a Bali-based bamboo design firm.

The roof of the Heart of School structure at Green School is shaped in the form of three nautiluses.

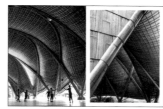

The Arc is a feat of engineering that required months of research and the fine-tuning of tailor-made details — a true testament to Ibuku's groundbreaking creativity and unparalleled design aesthetic. A structure of delicate beauty.

Yoga pavilion, designed by Ibuku, at Four Seasons Resort Bali at Sayan. The roof resembles a big leaf.

The uses for bamboo are limitless. Designers such as Ibuku and Faye Toogood demonstrate how bamboo can be manipulated to create stunning furniture and interiors.

Left: Private pool at Ananda House, which consists of three multi-level structures, at Green Village.

Right: The tallest bamboo structure in Bali, the six-level Sharma Springs was inspired by the petals of the lotus flower.

Left: Johnny Read, who introduced photographer Isabella Ginanneschi to the island of Bali.

Right: Plunge into the private pool at Ananda House.

A celebration of bamboo architecture, Green Village is filled with Ibuku-designed homes, many of which sit along the Ayung River.

Leaf House at Green Village, surrounded by the bamboo forest.

A bamboo hammock completes the master bedroom of River House at Green Village.

Stone-and-bamboo kitchen at Sunrise House at Green Village.

Left: A mango smoothie is the perfect refreshment to combat the warm climate.

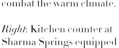

Right: Kitchen counter at Sharma Springs equipped with unique bamboo stools.

Left: The table is set for lunch at John Hardy's workshop in Ubud.

Right: Aura House is tucked within the shady forest, evoking a dramatic jungle fantasy.

Intricately woven bamboo ceiling in Aura House.

Discover the family-friendly River House at Green Village.

Craftsmanship, architecture and engineering merge to create artistic structures and patterns from bamboo.

A new vantage point awaits in the tree house at Bambu Indah.

Outdoor stone tub at Sharma Springs, the ideal destination for a romantic getaway.

Left: Nineteenth-century royal door restored by Kalpa Taru, which features scrolling lotus blossoms and diamond patterns.

Right: Bali provides numerous spaces to commune with nature.

Left: In the mountains of Munduk, Duma Cabin provides sweeping views of the valley.

Right: Boho-chic interior at the Island Houses in Seminyak.

The top floor of Cacao House is perfect for morning meditation or an afternoon yoga practice.

Ibuku's talented design team at their offices in Bali.

Left: Quaint sunroom, with woven-basketry screens, at Echo House.

Right: Kristina Melnikova in a campaign for clothing brand Palem, the Indonesian word for palm.

Millennium Bridge, one of the longest bamboo bridges in Asia, features a Minangkabau-inspired roof.

Kul Kul Bridge, the first structure built at Green School, connects the two parts of the campus.

John Hardy Workshop & Kapal Bamboo Boutique in Bali.

Furniture is seamlessly integrated into the architecture of Temple House at Green Village.

Left: Golden light streams through the window at Aura House.

Right: Natural pool in East Bali, one of the many natural wonders on the island.

In the far north of Bali, adventurers will come across the magical Aling Aling waterfall.

Left: Aerial view of Echo House on Ayung River.

Right: Ananda House surrounded by Bali's vibrant plant life.

Left: Artist Louise Despont and architect Alejandro Borrego at their Bali home.

Right: Edible and medicinal plants thrive in the pool area at Ananda House.

Left: Lounging in a caftan from Namu.

Right: The tree house at the Bambu Indah resort is a jungle getaway.

Left: Two-level pool at Four Seasons Resort Bali at Sayan.

Right: Julia Sullivan photographed in the fields of Bali for a Palem fashion campaign.

Secluded oasis in Bali's pristine environment at Amandari.

Diners at Seasalt, at Alila Manggis resort, enjoy their meals beside a tranquil lotus pond.

The wall panels in the bar at Kaum are imprinted with patterns from Torajan wood carvings.

Left: Traditional Balinese spread with satay.

Right: Dining table at Kaum, which allows guests to dine in the family-style of Indonesia's tribes.

Left: Custom creation by Bali-based Gaya Ceramic.

Right: Gold leaf and resin inlaid on a burnt-finished sculptural table — a custom design by Kalpa Taru.

Left: Namu's Tribal collection.

Right: Effortlessly chic Castro caftan by Namu.

Left: The main entrance of Desa Potato Head Beach Club was handcrafted by Make a Scene Bali.

Right: The expert weavers at Make a Scene Bali use traditional methods to create designs with coconut leaf.

Left: Portrait of a young Balinese woman, circa 1936.

Right: Saraswati Temple, known as the Ubud Water Palace, is notable for its lotus pond.

Bali boasts myriad waterfalls, including the Banyumala Twin Waterfalls.

Left: Tegenungan Waterfall in Bali.

Right: The Ayung River runs through the Green School campus, a private educational institution that promotes sustainability through learning in a natural environment.

Adventurers will enjoy the adrenaline rush of swinging up high among the jungle's treetops.

John Hardy campaign featuring his wife, Cynthia, and their daughters.

Left: Ananda House peaks through the tropical foliage.

Right: Traveling the roads of Sayan.

Left: A local sees to the day's tasks while Mount Agung, an active volcano in Bali, emits smoke.

Right: Namu's Andaman caftan photographed for *The Yak* magazine.

Left: Agriculture thrives in Bali's fertile soil and humid tropical climate.

Right: Workers in the Jatiluwih rice terraces.

The *subak* irrigation system, one of the most effective methods in the world for managing rice crops, ensures that all of Bali's rice fields receive their equal share of water.

Left: Rice paddy seen through a delicately carved window.

Right: Smiling local man in the rice fields of Bali.

Spectacular terraced rice fields in Bali, 1982.

Towering palm trees in front of a volcano in Bali.

Left: Celia Forner in the shade of a palm tree in Bali. Photographed by Ferdinando Scianna, 1989.

Right: Palm-tree fronds disperse rays of sunlight.

Left: Balinese residents prepare for the Usaba Dalem ceremony by installing *penjors*, decorated bamboo poles, along the roads.

Right: Artwork of a Balinese woman by Miguel Covarrubias graces the front cover of *Vanity Fair*, February 1936.

Bali's winding streets are dominated by overhanging trees and motorbikes.

Vendors selling their wares on the streets of Ubud.

Left: Sunrise at an Ubud market.

Right: Preparations are underway for the Galungan festival. Offerings are elaborate concoctions of incense, flowers, water and rice paste.

At the Pasar, by Indonesian painter Anak Agung Gde Sobrat.

Left: Bamboo forest in Penglipuran.

Right: Vivid colors in the coastal village of Tejakula.

Lauren Hutton, with Balinese dancers, on the steps of a temple in Ubud. Photographed by Arnaud de Rosnay for *Vogue*, 1970.

Left: Every detail at Desa Potato Head is intended to produce a world-class cultural experience.

Right: Fabrics used for *kebaya*, a traditional blouse, on display in Klungkung.

Geometric patterns and organic motifs adorn the clothing of Balinese women in Tenganan.

Women carrying rice and sugar to a Manusa Yadnya ceremony in Bali.

Left: Grandmother and grandson at the Tampaksiring market, also known as a *pasar*.

Right: Breakfast at a roadside *warung*, a small family-owned business.

All smiles during the morning commute in Denpasar.

Inside the studio of a Balinese artist in Batuan.

Left: The Batuan school of painting is distinguished by the crowded compositions.

Right: Sketching process.

Left: Handcrafted objects by Gaya Ceramic.

Right: Gaya Ceramic combines Italian flair with Balinese customs to produce home accessories such as ceramic flooring and wall coverings.

Single slab of rosewood with a bronze base sourced from Bandung, in West Java, and reworked by Kalpa Taru.

Bali is a haven for artisanal craftsmanship with brands such as Gaya Ceramic and Kalpa Taru creating products with mastery.

Left: Finely carved temple entrance with the head of Bhoma, a grotesque that is meant to protect against evil spirits.

Right: Team of highly skilled Balinese carvers.

Ulun Danu Temple complex on Lake Bratan, which provides water to the entire region, has shrines, known as *merus*, with pagoda-style thatched roofs.

Left: Hindu temples in Bali have open-air designs set within walled compounds.

Right: Lauren Hutton and Pilar Crespi on a motor scooter in the fields of Bali. Photographed by Arnaud de Rosnay for a *Vogue* fashion editorial, 1970.

Left: The bamboo bridge at Bambu Indah leads to numerous jungle adventures.

Right: Balinese long-tailed macaque at the Ubud Monkey Forest.

Left: Golden motifs decorate the entrance to Besakih Temple, the largest temple in Balinese Hinduism and also the most sacred.

Right: The Bali species of tiger is now extinct, but tigers can still be seen at Bali Zoo.

Tirta Empul, a Hindu Balinese water temple.

Left: Ganesha statues appear throughout Bali.

Right: *Petirtaan*, or bathing structure, with holy spring water at Tirta Empul Temple.

Left: Offerings to the gods at Tirta Empul Temple.

Right: Young Balinese dancers wearing ornate outfits.

Left: Balinese village market. Photographed by Henri Cartier-Bresson, 1949.

Right: Happy Balinese youth. Rice, which is a symbol of life in Balinese Hinduism, is placed on the forehead as a third eye.

Crowds converge in Gianyar for a royal funerary ceremony.

Left: Print by Tyra Kleen from *The Temple Dances in Bali*.

Right: Performers prepare for the Baris dance. Photographed by Henri Cartier-Bresson, 1949.

Traditional Balinese dance performance.

Left: Dance is a long-standing tradition in Balinese culture.

Right: Elaborate Balinese dance ensemble and fan.

Sculpture at a Balinese temple.

Left: Intricately decorated shrine in the Jeroan, or inner yard, at Tirta Empul Temple.

Right: Interior of Puri Saren Agung, also known as Ubud Palace.

Balinese *legong* dancers. *Legong* is characterized by expressive hand and arm movements, gestures of the face and head, and intricate footwork.

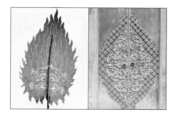

Left: Figure representing the god of fire to be used in *wayang kulit*, or a shadow-puppet play.

Right: Brightly colored carved door in Bali.

Stylish Balinese scene photographed by Ferdinando Scianna in Bali, 1989.

Left: Melasti, a purification ceremony, takes place on the beach and is meant to cleanse the world of suffering and bad things, throwing them into the ocean.

Right: Locals transport a funeral tower to the cemetery in Ubud, 1979.

Community performing a purification ceremony.

Left: Dress made of alang-alang.

Right: Woven crown, a traditional craft passed down from generation to generation.

Left: Private *kecak* dance around the bonfire.

Right: *Kecak* dancers commonly wear checked cloths around their waists.

Peaceful moment on the sands of Masceti Beach.

Left: Picturesque ride on the beach at sunset.

Right: Bali is simply paradise on Earth.

Left: Guests at Sunset Park, the rooftop bar at Desa Potato Head, enjoy a drink as the sun dips beyond the horizon.

Right: At Desa Potato Head, the Headstream streaming platform provides a global stage for upcoming talents, such as Dr. Yez.

Left: A round of sundowners at Sunset Park.

Right: Silhouette of an Indonesian fishing boat set against an orange-hued vista.

Author Elora Hardy with her mother, Penny Berton.

ACKNOWLEDGMENTS

The author sends love to all the wild and wonderful people who are making a future true to Bali's heart, and for that we must let our minds be flexible like bamboo.

The publisher would like to thank the following: Jennifer Carding, akg-images; Mary Ellen Jensen, Alamy Stock Photo; Reina Nakagawa, Art + Commerce; Joan Cargill, August Image; Thomas Haggerty, Bridgeman Images; Irina Nirland, Bukowskis; Gallery Stock; Irina Pampararo, Gaya Ceramic; Brian Stehlin, Getty Images; Isabella Ginanneschi; Bonnie Culbertson, Nyoman Widiantara, Green School Bali; Brian Hodges; Hans Hoefer; Agung Dwi Purnama, Septy Diantari, IBUKU; Polly Purser, Sri Utami, John Hardy; Avalon Carpenter, Kalpa Taru; Nathan Lawrence; Michael Shulman, Magnum Photos; Wayan Martino; Justin Misch, Morning of the Earth; Keiko Chiba, Nacása&Partners; Paola Zancanaro, NAMU; Melissa LeBoeuf, OTTO; Maria Garcia del Cerro, Potato Head; Suta Rahady; Tommaso Riva; Karine Bunout, Roger-Viollet; Cyril Saulnier; Ash Moros, Sebastian Faena Studio; Vincent Mounier, Shutterstock; Christin Markmann, Tim Street-Porter Studio; Anthony Tran, Trunk Archive; Annely Bouma, Claire Lebé-Violier, Viva Model Management; Alina Vlasova; Brent Smith, Walter Schupfer Management; Martin Westlake; Indra Wira; Zissou; Suki Zoë.

CREDITS

Assouline supports *One Tree Planted*
in its commitment to create a more
sustainable world through reforestation.

Front cover design: © Assouline Publishing.
Back cover tip-on (clockwise from top left): © Nathan
Lawrence; © Suki Zoë; © Nathan Lawrence; © Bruno Barbey/
Magnum Photos.
Endpages: © Colin Anderson Productions/Getty Images.

© 2022 Assouline Publishing
A Travel From Home™ Book
3 Park Avenue, 27th floor
New York, NY 10016 USA
Tel: 212-989-6769 Fax: 212-647-0005
assouline.com

Printed in Italy by Grafiche Milani, on Fedrigoni
Symbol Freelife paper, produced in Italy under the
strictest environmental standards.
ISBN: 9781649800473